Cambridge Experience Readers

Starter Level

Series editor: Nicholas Tims

Gone!

Margaret Johnson

CAMBRIDGE
UNIVERSITY PRESS

CAMBRIDGE
UNIVERSITY PRESS

University Printing House, Cambridge CB2 8BS, United Kingdom

One Liberty Plaza, 20th Floor, New York, NY 10006, USA

477 Williamstown Road, Port Melbourne, VIC 3207, Australia

314–321, 3rd Floor, Plot 3, Splendor Forum, Jasola District Centre, New Delhi – 110025, India

103 Penang Road, #05-06/07, Visioncrest Commercial, Singapore 238467

José Abascal 56, 1º – 28003 Madrid, Spain

Cambridge University Press is part of the University of Cambridge.

It furthers the University's mission by disseminating knowledge in the pursuit of education, learning and research at the highest international levels of excellence.

www.cambridge.org
Information on this title: www.cambridge.org/9788483235096

© Cambridge University Press 2009

This publication is in copyright. Subject to statutory exception and to the provisions of relevant collective licensing agreements, no reproduction of any part may take place without the written permission of Cambridge University Press.

First published 2009

40 39 38 37 36 35 34 33 32 31

Printed in Spain by Pulmen

ISBN 978-84-8323-509-6 Paperback; legal deposit: S.928-2009

No character in this work is based on any person living or dead. Any resemblance to an actual person or situation is purely accidental.

Illustrations by Lyn Knott

Audio recording by BraveArts, S.L.

Exercises by Peter McDonnell

The publishers are grateful to the following for permission to reproduce photographic material:

Getty Images | Timothy Allen for cover image

Contents

People in the story

Tom: a boy with a birthday
Mum: Tom's mother
Annie: Tom's sister
Dad: Tom's father
Neil: Tom's friend

BEFORE YOU READ

1 Look at the pictures in Chapter 1. What do you think?
Answer the questions.

1 How old is Tom?

....

2 Has Tom got a big sister?

....

3 Does Tom's mother work?

....

Birthday boy

'I'm sorry I'm working on your birthday, Tom.'

Tom's mother is leaving the house. She isn't looking at Tom. She's thinking about work.

'Have a nice day, love. See you tonight,' she says.

'Goodbye, Mum,' Tom says. He feels sad. He doesn't want her to go.

Tom's sister, Annie, comes down from her room. 'Happy birthday, little brother!' she says. 'Twelve today!'

Tom smiles. He likes being twelve.

'Can I give you your birthday present[1] this afternoon?' Annie asks. 'I'm going shopping this morning with my friends.' She goes to the door.

'I want to go shopping,' Tom starts to say, but Annie doesn't hear.

'Enjoy your birthday,' she says. Then she leaves too.

Now Tom's father is the only person at home[2]. Tom finds him at his desk. He's working on his computer. Tom's father works at home, and he works all the time. Tom walks into his father's office and his father turns and looks at him. 'Hello, Tom,' he says. 'What are you going to do with your birthday money?'

'I don't know, Dad,' Tom says. 'Can we go shopping?'

Tom's father is looking at his computer again. 'Not today, Tom,' he says. 'I must finish this work. Where's Annie?'

'She's shopping with her friends,' Tom says.

He knows his father isn't listening. He's reading an email on his computer.

'That's nice,' he says, but he doesn't look at Tom. 'Have a good time!'

'OK,' says Tom and he leaves the room.

Tom phones his friend Neil. Neil's mother answers.

'Can I speak to Neil?' Tom asks.

'I'm sorry,' Neil's mother says. 'He's playing football in Winston Park³. Is that Tom?'

'Yes,' says Tom.

'Neil tells me it's your birthday today,' Neil's mother says. 'Happy birthday!'

'Thank you,' says Tom.

'I must go, but have a good day!' says Neil's mother.

'Thank you,' Tom says again and he puts the phone down.

'No one has any time for me today,' he thinks. 'It's my birthday and no one has any time for me.'

LOOKING BACK

1 Check your answers to *Before you read* on page 4.

ACTIVITIES

2 Complete the sentences with the names in the box.

> Tom (x3)   Mum   Dad   Annie (x2)   Neil (x2)

1 _Mum_ leaves the house and goes to work.
2 .... is Tom's sister.
3 It's ....'s birthday.
4 .... is twelve today.
5 .... is going shopping.
6 .... works at home.
7 .... is Tom's friend.
8 .... is at the park.
9 .... isn't happy.

3 Underline the correct words in each sentence.
1 Mum is thinking about *her work* / *Tom's birthday*.
2 Annie *has* / *hasn't* got a present for Tom.
3 Tom's *father* / *mother* has got a computer.
4 Tom *has got some* / *hasn't got any* birthday money.
5 Tom's father *can* / *can't* go shopping.
6 Dad is *listening to Tom* / *reading his email*.
7 Tom speaks to *Neil* / *Neil's mother*.
8 Neil *knows* / *doesn't know* it's Tom's birthday.

10

4 Who do the underlined words refer to in these lines from the text?

> Annie (x2)   Tom   Dad
>
> Mum   Tom and Dad   Neil

1 'See <u>you</u> tonight.' (page 5) .... *Tom* ....

2 He doesn't want <u>her</u> to go. (page 6) ....

3 <u>She</u> goes to the door. (page 7) ....

4 Tom finds <u>him</u> at his desk. (page 7) ....

5 'Can <u>we</u> go shopping?' (page 8) ....

6 'She's shopping with <u>her</u> friends.' (page 8) ....

7 '<u>He</u>'s playing football in Winston Park.' (page 9) ....

5 Match the questions with the answers.

1 Why is today a special day for Tom? ☐ *b*

2 What has Tom got for his birthday? ☐

3 What does Tom's dad do at home? ☐

4 Who does Tom talk to on the phone? ☐

5 Who is playing football? ☐

a He works.

~~b~~ It's his birthday.

c Neil's mother.

d He's got money.

e Neil.

LOOKING FORWARD

6 Tick (✓) what you think happens in Chapter 2.

1 Tom goes to the park. ☐

2 Tom stays at home. ☐

Chapter 2

The camera

Tom leaves the house and walks to Winston Park. He doesn't like football, but he wants to be with people.

It's a hot day. In Winston Park there are lots of mothers and fathers with their children. Boys and girls are running and laughing. Everyone looks happy. Tom sees Neil and some more boys. They're playing football.

Tom goes over. Neil sees him. He smiles. 'Hello, Tom!' he calls. 'Happy birthday!'

'Thank you!' Tom calls, but Neil is running to get the ball.

Tom watches the game[4] for ten minutes, but Neil doesn't speak to him again. Neil's good at football and he's enjoying the game. Tom starts walking across Winston Park.

He sits down on a seat and takes a drink from his bag.

He puts his bag down. There is another bag under the seat.

'What's this?' thinks Tom. The bag is black. Tom opens it. He's looking for a name. There is only one thing in the bag: a camera.

Tom takes it out. Then he looks in the bag again, but there is nothing in it. No name.

Tom looks at the camera. There are four buttons: PHOTO, DELETE, ON and OFF.

Tom puts his finger on the ON button and presses[5] it. The camera makes a noise.

The black bag is on the seat. Tom can see it in the camera. Tom puts his finger on the PHOTO button. He presses it. The camera makes another noise. Tom looks at the photo of the bag. It's OK, but he doesn't want a photo of a bag, so he presses the DELETE button. The photo goes away.

'This camera is OK,' Tom thinks. 'But it isn't my camera. I must take it to the police. I can buy a camera with my birthday money.'

Tom puts out his hand to take the camera bag from the seat. But the bag isn't there.

He looks under the seat. No bag. He looks behind the seat. No bag. Tom doesn't understand. 'Where is the bag?' he thinks.

A squirrel runs in front of the seat. Tom wants a photo of it. The squirrel stops.

'It's looking for food,' Tom thinks. He smiles and presses the PHOTO button. But when he looks at the photo, it isn't good.

'Squirrels are too fast for photos,' Tom thinks.

He presses the DELETE button. The photo of the squirrel goes away.

When Tom looks for the squirrel, he can't see it.

'Squirrels run fast,' Tom thinks. 'But not that fast. Where is it?'

Tom looks at the camera. He doesn't understand. Something is wrong. He wants to try the camera again. There are some flowers next to his seat. Tom looks at the camera again. He can see the flowers. He presses the PHOTO button and takes a photo of the flowers.

Then he presses the DELETE button to make the photo go away. Tom takes the camera away from his face. He looks for the flowers. They aren't there.

'The flowers are gone,' he thinks. 'Gone!'

LOOKING BACK

1 Check your answer to *Looking forward* on page 11.

ACTIVITIES

2 <u>Underline</u> the correct words in each sentence.
1 Tom <u>*wants*</u> / *doesn't want* to be with friends.
2 Tom *plays football with* / *talks to* Neil.
3 Neil *is* / *isn't* good at football.
4 Tom has something to *eat* / *drink* in the park.
5 *Tom* / *Neil* finds a camera.
6 Tom *uses* / *doesn't use* the camera.
7 Tom wants to take the camera *to the police* / *home*.
8 Tom deletes *all* / *some of* his photos.

3 Put the sentences in order.
1 Tom finds a camera. ☐
2 Tom speaks to Neil. ☐
3 Tom sits down. ☐
4 Tom goes to the park. ☐*1*
5 Tom deletes the photo. ☐
6 Tom watches the game. ☐
7 Tom takes a photo of the bag. ☐
8 The bag is gone. ☐

4 Are the sentences true (*T*) or false (*F*)?

1 Tom runs to the park. ☐ F
2 The weather is good. ☐
3 Tom doesn't watch all the game. ☐
4 Tom finds a blue bag under his seat. ☐
5 There's nothing in the bag. ☐
6 The camera has got three buttons. ☐
7 Tom takes a photo of his bag. ☐
8 Tom doesn't like his photo of the squirrel. ☐

5 Answer the questions.

1 Does Tom like football?

....

2 Where does Tom find the bag?

....

3 What does he look for in the bag?

....

4 Is the picture of the squirrel good? Why / Why not?

....

LOOKING FORWARD

6 Tick (✓) what you think happens in the next two chapters.

1 Tom plays football. ☐
2 Tom takes more photos with the camera. ☐
3 Tom goes shopping. ☐

Chapter 3

Where's the ball?

Tom puts the camera down. He doesn't want it in his hands now. He feels afraid⁶.

He thinks about the camera bag, the squirrel and the flowers.

'When I take photos of things with this camera, they go away,' he thinks. 'I don't know how, but they do.'

Across Winston Park he can see the boys playing football.

'I must tell Neil about this!' he thinks. He puts the camera in his bag and starts running across the park.

But after a minute he stops running. He thinks about the camera bag, the squirrel and the flowers. He's near the boys now.

'It's my birthday,' he thinks. 'I want Neil to come to the shops with me. We can get a pizza. I can buy something with my birthday money.'

A boy in a blue T-shirt has the ball now. He's running fast. Then everyone shouts.

'Goal!'

Lots of the boys run to the boy in the blue T-shirt. They are all very happy.

Tom quickly takes the camera from the bag and looks into it. He can see the ball.

He presses the PHOTO button and then the DELETE button. The boys want to start playing again.

'Hey!' shouts the boy in the blue T-shirt. 'Where's the ball?'

No one can understand. They look on the grass[7] and
behind trees.

'Can you see the ball, Tom?' Neil asks.

'No, sorry,' Tom says. 'I don't know where the ball
is. I don't think you can play now. Do you want to get
a pizza with me? I can buy something to eat with my
birthday money.'

But Neil doesn't hear Tom. He's listening to the boy in the blue T-shirt.

'It's OK,' he says. 'I've got another ball in my bag.'

'Good,' says Neil. 'But where is our other ball?'

'I don't know,' says the boy.

He gets the new ball from his bag. They start to play again.

Tom thinks about taking a new photo: a photo of the new ball. But the boys run away across the grass and Tom turns and starts to walk home.

Chapter 4

The computer

When Tom gets home, his father is making a coffee.

'Tom? Is that you?' he calls.

'Yes,' Tom answers.

'Do you want a coffee?' his father asks.

'No thank you,' answers Tom. 'I'm just getting something from my room.'

Tom quickly runs up to his father's office. It's the room with the computer. He takes the camera from his bag. He can see the computer in it. He quickly presses PHOTO. Then DELETE.

He looks at the table. No computer.

'Good,' he thinks.

Tom's father comes into the room with his coffee. He smiles at Tom.

'OK?' he asks. Then he stops smiling. 'Where's my computer?' he asks.

'I don't know,' says Tom.

'I don't understand,' Tom's father says. 'Where is it?'
He looks behind Tom. He looks under the table. He
looks all over the room. Then he looks at Tom.

'Tom?' he says. 'Where's my computer?'

'I don't know,' answers Tom.

'Computers don't just go!' Tom's father says.

'Yes they do!' thinks Tom.

Then he looks at his father. 'Can we go to the shops, Dad?' he asks.

'No, Tom!' his father says. 'I must find my computer! I'm going to phone the police.'

'After the police come,' Tom says, 'can we go to the shops then?'

But Tom's father can't stop thinking about his computer.

'Please, Tom,' he says. He looks tired. 'I know it's your birthday, but all my work is on that computer. It's very important. I don't know what to do.'

Tom looks at his father.

'I'm sorry, Dad,' he says.

His father smiles a little. 'It's OK, son,' he says. 'Go and enjoy your birthday.'

Tom leaves the room. 'I can't enjoy my birthday,' he thinks. 'No one has any time for me.'

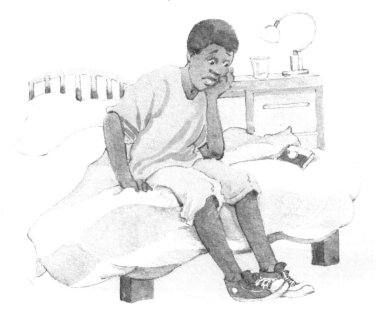

Tom goes to his room and sits on his bed. Then he thinks about his mother and he knows what he wants to do.

LOOKING BACK

1 Check your answer to *Looking forward* on page 23.

ACTIVITIES

2 <u>Underline</u> the correct words in each sentence.
  1 Tom *tells / <u>doesn't tell</u>* his friend about the camera.
  2 Tom wants to *eat something / play football* with Neil.
  3 Tom takes a photo of the *ball / boy*.
  4 The boys continue playing with *a new / the old* ball.
  5 Tom *takes / doesn't take* a photo of the new ball.
  6 Tom's dad is *working / making a drink* when Tom gets home.
  7 When Tom gets home, he goes to his *bedroom / dad's office*.
  8 Tom's dad's computer is important because it has a lot of *work / photos* on it.
  9 Tom *is / isn't* enjoying his birthday.

3 Answer the questions.
  In Chapters 3 and 4, who ...
  1 is afraid? _____Tom_____
  2 asks Tom about the ball? _____
  3 finds another ball in his bag? _____
  4 makes a drink? _____
  5 loses his computer? _____
  6 can't do any work? _____
  7 wants to go shopping? _____
  8 isn't happy? _____

4 Match the two parts of the sentences.

1 Tom runs across the park because $\boxed{c}$
2 Tom doesn't take a photo of the new ball because $\square$
3 Tom's dad isn't in his office because $\square$
4 Tom wants the computer to go away because $\square$
5 Tom can't enjoy his birthday because $\square$

a he's making a coffee.
b no one has any time for him.
$\cancel{c}$ he wants to tell Neil about the camera.
d he wants to go shopping with his dad.
e the boys run away.

5 Answer the questions.

1 Why does Tom put the camera down at the start of Chapter 3?

....

2 What does Tom want to do with his birthday money?

....

3 How many photos does Tom take in Chapters 3 and 4?

....

LOOKING FORWARD

6 Tick (✓) what you think happens in the next chapter.

1 Tom goes to see his mum at work. $\square$
2 He takes the camera to the police. $\square$
3 He buys a new camera. $\square$

Chapter 5

Trying to help

Tom leaves the house and walks to his mother's café – Kathy's Coffee Shop.

The café sells food all day. Lots of people go there on Saturdays. Tom can see his mother in the café. She looks hot. There are people at all the tables and they're all waiting for their food.

'Mum's tired,' Tom thinks. 'She works a lot.'

He goes into the café.

His mother sees him.

'Hello, Tom,' she says. 'Why are you here on your birthday?'

'I'm here to help you,' he says.

His mother smiles.

'Oh, thank you, Tom,' she says. 'People want plates and cups for their food and drinks,' she says. 'They're all dirty.'

She takes Tom to the dirty plates and cups in the kitchen[8].

'Can you wash them for me?' she asks.

Tom smiles.

'Of course,' he says.

Tom's mother smiles again.

'You're a good boy,' she says. Then she leaves the kitchen.

Tom quickly takes the camera from his bag.

'I can have an afternoon with Mum,' he thinks. 'We can go to a restaurant. Or watch a film.'

He can see the dirty cups and plates in the camera. He presses PHOTO. Then DELETE. Then he takes the camera away and looks.

'Gone,' he thinks. 'They're gone.' And he smiles.

His mother comes back into the kitchen. She looks all over the room.

'Tom?' she says. 'Where are the cups and plates?'

Tom thinks for a few⁹ seconds.

'It's the camera,' he tells her. 'When I take a photo, things go away.'

His mother looks at him. She looks very tired now. 'What?' she asks. 'I don't understand.'

'The camera ...' Tom starts, but his mother speaks.

'Tom,' she says, 'there aren't any plates or cups and there are lots of people in the café. What am I going to do?'

'Close the café, Mum,' Tom says. 'We can go out.'

His mother is angry now.

'I can't close the café, Tom!' she says. 'This is my job! Now, please, tell me where the cups and plates are.'

'I don't know, Mum,' Tom starts saying. 'It's the camera ...'

The door opens. Tom's sister comes in.

'Hello,' she says. 'What's wrong?'

Tom's mother starts telling Annie about the plates and cups, but Annie isn't listening. She sees Tom's camera.

'What's this?' she says and takes it from her brother. 'Is it new?'

'Give it to me!' Tom says.

Annie doesn't listen. She puts the camera to her eye. She looks at Tom.

'Smile!' she says.

'No!' Tom shouts.
Annie presses the PHOTO button.
'Give the camera to me, Annie!' Tom shouts.
Annie looks at the photo.

'This isn't a good photo of you, Tom,' Annie says.
'No! Don't press any buttons!' shouts Tom.
But it's too late. Annie presses DELETE.

LOOKING BACK

. . . .

1 Check your answer to *Looking forward* on page 37.

ACTIVITIES

. . . .

2 Put the sentences in order.
1 Tom and his mum go into the kitchen. ☐
2 Annie takes the camera from Tom. ☐
3 Tom takes a photo of the cups and plates. ☐
4 Annie takes a photo of Tom. ☐
5 Tom goes to his mum's work. ☐1☐
6 Tom tells his mum about the camera. ☐
7 Annie arrives at the café. ☐
8 The cups and plates go away. ☐

3 Match the two parts of the sentences.
1 Tom goes to the café because ☐d☐
2 Tom takes a photo of the cups and plates because ☐
3 Tom's mum wants the cups and plates because ☐
4 Tom's mum is angry because ☐
5 Annie presses DELETE because ☐

a the cups and plates are gone.
b it isn't a good photo of Tom.
c there are lots of people in the café.
d~~ he wants to go out with his mum.
e he doesn't want to wash them.